A glance back ⟨

Bream

Chestnut Avenue circa 1930, before the road was made up. The Countess Dunraven of Clearwell, who had Clearwell church rebuilt on its present site and also restored the village cross, is said to have ordered the planting of this avenue of trees around 1870.

by
Ruth Proctor Hirst

Black Dwarf Publications

Acknowledgements

Thanks for information and loan of photographs to Mrs. Hazel Hirst, Clarence James, David Rudge, Harold Phillips, Averil Kear, Melville Watts, David Wilks, Cyril Edwards, Brian Johns, Marina Lambert, Geoff & Diane Watkins and Neil Parkhouse.

Lower village from Buck's Meadow in 1907, with St James' church on the left and the vicarage in the trees beyond. The Coleford to Lydney road cuts through the centre, with the cottages of St James' Square just to the right of it in the middle and Ferndale Cottage right behind them. On the skyline, top right, the house partly hidden by the stone barn is The Hollies, a Young Ladies Academy in 1878 and in the 1930s where the Misses Trewin and Nancy Pearce ran their dressmaking business.

British Library Cataloguing-in-Publication Data. A catlogue record for this book is available from the British Library
ISBN 0 9533028 3 0

Black Dwarf Publications
47 – 49 high Street, Lydney, Gloucestershire GL15 5DD

Printed by M.D. Jenkins Ltd.,
Unit 53/54, Lydney Trading Estate, Harbour Road, Lydney, Gloucestershire GL15 4EJ

~A short history of Bream ~

Bream is the largest village in the Forest of Dean – indeed, some say it is the largest village in England. It is certainly a very sprawling place, consisting of the early village around the Maypole and the church, Bream's Eaves, Bream Woodside, The Tufts (Bream Meend), Brockhollands, Mill Hill and Parkend Road.

Although the village as we know it today began life around the church, the very early beginnings of a community here can be found in the fields either side of Bream Avenue, between Breams Cross Farm and Noxon, where flint and other prehistoric artefacts have been found by members of the local archaeological group who field-walked them with permission of the landowners. The Silures, who lived in the Forest area, were first to mine the iron ore and the area was later known to the Romans, who also exploited the mineral deposists, leaving as their legacy the well-known Scowles, in the Devil's Chapel, part of the Lydney Park estate.

A clearing *'called Bream (Bremereude) had been made'*, according to the Regard of 1282 when the Forest was being checked, and it is known that land at Bream had been cleared and settled by the mid 14th century. Mention is made too, in 1301-2, as to the

Crown possessing the right of conferring the tithes of the 'assarted' (encroaching) Forest lands not being within the bounds of the adjacent churches. The King, Edward I, decided the claim in favour of the church of Newland, to whom a considerable proportion of the existing encroachments, including those reputedly the oldest, paid tithes. A list of such by Reverend Nicholls includes lands near Paster, Nels and Whitecroft, containing 507 acres, and land near Bream, 213 acres.

At Bream, which was referred to at this date as a tithing of Newland on the road between there and Lydney, five or more dwellings were recorded by 1462 and, although no actual date is known for its original erection, a chapel of ease, dedicated to St. James, existed before 1505. It was either repaired or rebuilt later, when it was reseated by Thomas Donning in 1618. Henry Bream was recorded in 1537 as *'having custody of Le Gawle Wood'* – Gablewood (*Gawle* – Gaveller) – whilst John Morgan of Bryeme (Bream) had been a steward of the Queen's (Elizabeth I) Court of St. Briavels in 1592.

Much of the surrounding Forest had been denuded of trees by Sir John Wintour and others during the Civil War and eventually enclosures were set up,

A glimpse inside the Devil's Chapel around 1907. Part of the Lydney Park estate, it is the result of iron ore mining during the time of the Romans, the great holes left in the rocks being gradually covered by trees and luxuriant undergrowth.

in order to allow regeneration of the timber lost. However, the local population, used to running their animals freely, were not happy with the idea, feeling they were being penalised. Matters came to a head in 1831, when a party under the leadership of Warren James of Bream, after giving notice of their intentions, broke down the fences and let their animals in. The militia were called in and, after a brief period, the rioters gave up. Many were caught but James managed to evade capture and hid in a mine nearby, being fed by local folk. Unfortunately for him, a reward was offered and, in those hard-up times, it proved too much for one local who, on the pretext of taking him food, led the soldiers to his hiding place. He was taken to Coleford and then on to Gloucester, where he was at first sentenced to death, although this was later commuted to transportation to Australia. Some years later a pardon was sent out but apparently nothing more was heard of him. Some of the enclosure banks can still be seen and in the Bream's Eaves Enclosure is a stone erected in 1844 recording its details; '11a. 3r. 23p'. 'Lincoln C. Commr.' – i.e. 11 acres 3 roods 23 perches in size, as under Crown Commissioner Lincoln.

Most householders had their piece of garden, their pig, perhaps a cow and a few sheep and, with the many geese and fowl which roamed the numerous greens around the village, this helped to keep them fairly self sufficient. Until quite recently there were still several greens in the village but except for Woodside, Old Hang and the green down Whitecroft Road, now a children's playground, the others have all been built over.

Of the farms, Court Farm on the Coleford road is a 17th century building in the ownership of the Wildin family, who can trace their ancestry back over six hundred years to a High Constable of St. Briavels, circa the 13th century. Pastor's Hill, Brockhollands and Bream's Cross Farms are also ancient, the first being also of the 17th century, though legend has it that it was built on the site of one of King John's hunting lodges. In the 17th century it belonged to the Gough family, a member of which also owned the New Inn, or The Old House, as it was known, and which is situated at the Maypole. At present it is being restored by Mr. Bill Parker of Stowe, who also owns the Flour Mill Colliery engine house where he carries out the restoration of old steam engines. Brockhollands, recorded in 1578, was the home of the Wintour family. Bream Cross Farm, by the ancient portway to Bearse Farm, St. Briavels, stands at the Bream end of The Avenue and a date stone of 1565 which was originally there, denotes yet another ancient site. In 1671 Thomas Byrkin and his son Richard lived there; in the late 19th century the farmer was James Hughes, with the Gunter family there in the 1930s and it is now owned by Mr G. Reeks. The house was reputed to be a halting place for coaches and on the lawn in front of it, forming a raised garden feature, is the top of the chimney stack from the Parkend Ironworks, which was felled in 1908.

Another important estate is that of Prior's or Bream Lodge, situated on the boundary between Bream and Aylburton, on the road to St. Briavels. It was part of the Forest waste assarted and allowed by the Crown to Llanthony Priory in the 14th century. Through the centuries, it has been owned by various gentry including Powletts, Lawrences and Josiah Verelst. The latter, who died in 1819, lies in a tomb in Newland church. During the 1930s and early 1940s, Major and Mrs Percival resided there and the grounds would be opened up for the village fetes, when one could walk around the lake. The house has been altered and enlarged over the years, with pediments on the east and west frontages added in the late 18th century. The owner is now Mr Melville Watts of Lydney.

Other farms around the village include Kingsmoor (on the Lydney road), Pathwell and Saunders Green. The latter, with Brockhollands, were once part of the Pastor's Hill estate. The Gorsty mesne, opposite the entrance to Kingsmoor Farm (now called Treetops Farm), became a pig farm in the 1960s, when Mr Johnson of Redhill Pig Farm, Lydney, purchased the ground. It was later sold to a Mr. Richards, still as a pig farm, and eventually closed down about 1989. For some years it remained empty until, in late 1997/early 1998, the buildings were demolished and chicken-rearing sheds erected soon after. To date, there has been controversy surrounding this, due to the overwhelming stench which emanates from it at various times.

Successive clergymen have left their mark on the design of the present church. The Rev. Henry Poole is said to have hauled the first load of stone for the rebuilding of St. James, Bream, on the same day that St. Paul's, Parkend, was consecrated – 25 April 1822. The Crown gave £50 towards the restoration and the rebuilt church was consecrated on 13 October 1826, as was the old churchyard. In 1861, the Rev. Cornelius Witherby (1858-68) made further alterations; the nave was lengthened, the north aisle and arcade erected, the chancel enlarged, and the tower which Poole had put up, with its winding stair and short spire, removed and the present bell turret put in its place. The piscena arch, unusually high at the east end of the north wall of the chancel (where it was moved to from the south wall in 1861 to make room for the south east and east windows and door), is cut out of one stone and rests on a through stone, the drain being plugged. The stone, similar to that of the oldest parts of the church and possibly part of the original chapel, is thought to date from between 1300 and 1500.

This did not mark the end of alterations; the Rev. Henry Edward Dandy (1883-96) moved the old porch from the middle of the south wall to its present position, the old vestry was demolished and the north aisle extended to form the new vestry and organ chamber. The Rev. George Cass (1902-19) completely reseated the church and also gave the reredos, in memory of his father George Granger Cass, who died in 1905. A lady chapel was installed at the east end of the north aisle; it was a gift of the parochial Guild of St. Mary.

Disaster overtook St. James's church one July evening in 1981, when fire broke out due to an electrical fault in the organ. The vestry and east end of the church suffered great damage and, when it reopened in 1983, the interior had been much modernised. During the months of closure, services were held in the Maypole garage car showroom, opposite the church, thanks to the owner Mr Brian Franklin.

Non conformist meetings were recorded in the parochial lands of Bream and Yorkley in the early 1800s, with the Bible Christians, Primitive Methodists and Wesleyans all building places of worship in the 1850s and 60s. The Bible Christians had visited many places in the Forest, establishing small societies in various hamlets including Bream, services being held there from 1841. Later, in 1851, they built a chapel on the Parkend Road. The mission became a separate circuit in 1858 and in the following year the chapel was rebuilt, including a schoolroom. It was again rebuilt in 1906, as was the old schoolroom alongside it.

There was a decline in numbers over the following decades at all three chapels in the village, Wesleyan, Woodside and the Primitive Methodists at Bream's Eaves. After a lot of heart searching, Wesley eventually closed in 1959 and the members transferred to Parkend Road, the two village congregations joining as one.

The Wesleyans were holding services at Bream's Eaves by 1851, with an average attendance of 100, moving to a new chapel at Bream Woodside in 1860. Additions to it were made in 1913, including a schoolroom and vestry. The chapel became part of the Methodist Church in 1932 and remained in use until 1959, when it finally closed and the remaining membership joined with the Parkend Road society. It became a Pentecostal church in 1964.

The Hirst family – John Edwin, of Pastor's Hill, and his brother Frank Bert, of the Shop, Parkend Road, along with the latter's wife Elizabeth, sons the late Alan, Robert and his wife Hazel – have been very much involved with the life and work of both places of worship, having moved with the rest of the congregation. A font, given in memory of another son David, who died young, was transferred by invitation from Wesley and installed in the present building. Gladys Hirst, daughter of John, was the first to be married at Wesley, in 1919, her father having had it licensed specially for the occasion, when she wed the Rev. Albert Jones OBE. Frank and Alan were much concerned with the local cricket team whilst, in the 1930s, John gave the chapel members free use of a tennis court and cricket pitch laid out at Pastor's Hill.

The Primitive Methodists formed a society in 1851 at Bream's Eaves, building a chapel there in 1858. Alterations were made in 1903 and a schoolroom was added. It also became part of the Methodist Church in 1932 and finally closed in 1991. It was taken over a couple of years later by St. James' church and opened up as The Eaves Centre, both as a church and a meeting place, and on Tuesdays it also becomes a Coffee shop.

All that remains of Ranters Green, showing the Primitive Methodist chapel and schoolroom, now The Eaves Centre. So many of the greens have been built on since the end of World War Two.

Mary Gough of Pastor's Hill who, with her husband James had been benefactors of the church, left £50 upon her death in 1700 to buy land, the profit from which was to be used to teach poor children of Bream tithing. By 1712, another benefaction had been joined to her gift and 23 children were being taught.

The Rev. Henry Poole established a school on the National Plan for Bream children in 1830. This was situated near Bream Tufts and, in 1847, 80 children were being taught there. However, even with help from the Crown and the Gough charity, Poole was making up the deficiency in running costs himself, due to the poverty the area was then suffering from. This situation could not continue, however, and in 1862 the Rev. Cornelius Witherby moved the school to a site at Bream's Eaves, considered to be more central for the growing village. This new National School and schoolhouse were provided with financial help from Alice Davies, also a great benefactor to the church, where the vestry and organ chamber were erected in her memory in 1891.

The C of E School, formerly the National, was enlarged in 1893 and 1900 but was still overcrowded in 1904 with an attendance of 382. To help ease the problem, an Infants department was opened opposite the main school. In 1910, this new building was named Bream Council School and had an average attendance of 311. This Council School was enlarged in 1912 and 1927, when it was reorganised to take junior girls and infants, leaving the C of E with the junior boys.

In 1951 the C of E School, which had accepted Controlled Status in 1948, became a junior mixed school. At the same time, the girls' department in the Council School was converted to a Secondary Modern School, which later closed in 1973. Over 200 pupils were then transferred to schools in Lydney and Five Acres, the C of E School moving into the Secondary School buildings. In 1992, with 222 children on its roll, it was renamed Bream C of E (Voluntary Controlled) Primary School, whilst the old boys' school was converted to a youth centre and county library at the same time. In 1998, the future of this latter, now the Community Centre, was in some doubt and closure was being talked of. Howver, due to the overwhelming response to this threat, this has been deferred although, at the time of writing, its future had still not been settled happily.

Bream's oldest surviving public house is The Rising Sun, although now renamed The Village Inn. It stands near the Sun Green, site of the War Memorial, and would have been near the edge of the original village. It was the meeting place for a Friendly Society in 1787. In the High street, The Two Swans was noted in 1869, with The King's Head at Bream Woodside, The Miners' Rest at Bream Meend, and the Miners' Arms, later The Winding Wheel and now flats, on the Coleford road all in the late 1870s.

Also, at the Maypole, were The Dolphin Inn and the Live and Let Live, as well as the New Inn by 1814 and the Cross Keys by 1792. The latter moved to a building near Parkend Road which had been built as a gents' outfitters and later became Mullan's dentist's surgery. By late 1998, it was still open but had changed its name to The Hedgehog! With the exception of the Rising Sun/Village Inn, all of the others have closed and are now private houses. Oakwood mill, recorded as a mill from 1520, using steam power in 1885 and closed by 1900, later became The Oakwood Mill Inn but closed sometime in the 1960s/70s and it too is now a private house. The Maypole itself, a notable landmark which stood at the junction of High Street and the Lydney to Coleford road, was cut down circa 1925 because it had become a traffic hazard.

The rather scattered village of the 18th century and earlier gradually became more integrated during the 19th century, as houses were erected on such places as Mill Hill, The Tufts, Woodside and Bream's Eaves. By the turn of the century, many more houses and shops had appeared, including Manchester House, the school, Macfarlane's and also the Co-op, which stood on the corner of Whitecroft Road and is now flats. After the First World War council houses were built on the open parts of the village at Highbury and Parkend Road. Following the Second World War, more infilling occurred, with estates not only on the old greens but on the fields behind the New Inn too (where fairs and circuses were once held), now called Maypole Green. Highbury Avenue was also extended, with houses built on the fields of High Beech Farm.

Over the years it has been interesting to see how the various types of business in Bream grew, expanded and changed, although sobering when one realises that they have latterly almost all vanished, victims of better transport and the growth of the supermarkets. Before the Second World War, small shops could be found scattered all around the village, attached to ordinary houses, in many cases being the front room given over to trade. They sold anything and everything the nearby inhabitants could need or afford. Prior to this, pedlars would have come round at certain times with their various wares and it was up to the housewife to keep in a good stock of the necessities. Before the First World War, there was an old man from Abergavenny who used to come through the Sunday afternoon in September before Gloucester 'Mop' with his pack of home-made sweets, these being his wares to sell there. Weights and measures must have been of some dubiety and there is a record of Richard James of Bream being fined at the Forest Quarter Sessions in September 1807 for using faulty weights.

Among the many self-sufficient tradesmen were the blacksmiths and, in 1851, four were listed for the village. There were also six shoemakers and six carpenters, plus their respective labourers but only two grocers, Richard T. Heighway and Richard Morgan. A few years later, in 1889, there were several more, including Macfarlane's, Hirst Bros. and Mrs Mountjoy, as well as Mr Heighway although Morgan had gone. The boot and shoe makers were still very much in evidence, as were the blacksmiths and dressmakers. By 1863, Richard Heighway was also the postmaster as well as general grocer and linen draper. In 1899, Albert J. Batten was listed as the post master, a position he held until at least 1919, being succeeded by Henry Gatfield who was recorded as being at the post office in 1923. Mrs Gatfield (Henry's widow) and her daughter ran it during the 1930s and later Mr and Mrs Selby were in charge. It was in premises through this period by the Miners' Welfare Hall in the High Street, just opposite Highbury Avenue (Piano Street!). This post office eventually closed in the late 1980s and is now occupied by Bream Auto Store. At the beginning of the 1990s, a new post office was opened at Family Affair, a ladies fashion shop, on Brockhollands Road. It also became a Police Information Point (PIP) in late 1998, as there is now no resident police station. The Miners' Welfare Hall is now Bream Rugby Club but was a cinema from before WW2 to just after.

The police station at the Maypole end of the High Street in the 1930s. P.C. Beddis, on the right, and another officer stand outside the building, which had originally been occupied by Richard Heighways' store – the alterations to the frontage are apparent. Note the 'Gloucestershire Police Station' plaque above the door and the 'Wanted' poster on the noticeboard.
Photo courtesy Gloucestershire Record Office

The first police station was in a building just above the New Inn, before it was moved to the corner house where Richard Heighway had his shop. Latterly, it moved again, to a modern house on Parkend Road, PC Andy Barrow being the last resident policeman. The sub post office which served the Parkend Road area for many years also closed in 1994, despite local opposition. The building which is currently occupied by Robin's Nest was Williams & Cotton's grocery store in the 1930s and later it became Miles Merchants. Prior to the First World War, one end of it had housed a branch of the Capital & Counties (later Lloyd's) Bank.

The roads in the Forest of Dean before the turnpike era were probably no better or worse than in other parts of the country but, with the various Acts passed in the 18th and 19th centuries, they were improved and new ones made. That between Bream and Parkend, with its toll house at the junction with the Coleford road, was made in 1828, while the one between Bream and Yorkley was not made until after 1859. The Pike House, which used to stand opposite the Bream Cricket Club, and the Hard-up Tree at the crossroads (where the colliers would congregate when there was no work – hence its name) have both been swept away in the name of progress. To evade paying tolls at this point, the carriers used a track leading off some way down Mill Hill, travelling out across to the Tufts and on to Bream Cross Farm. Two other toll houses were situated locally, one at Trowgreen and the other at Sling (Clay Lane End).

Though even some of the outlying lanes are now good roads, in the past they were merely dirt tracks – very wet and muddy in the winter, and dusty in the summer. They were used by the miners and colliers, and others, on their way to and from work. The surfaces of the 'made' roads were produced with layers of large stones, which were broken up by hand, following which dirt would be tipped on top and rolled in to make a firm surface. In later years, they were repaired by having hot tar sprayed over them, stone or gravel then being spread on this by hand and packed down with the aid of a steamroller.

The main occupations of the inhabitants of Bream were iron and coal mining, quarrying and farming. There were iron ore mines all round the area, including in the Devil's Chapel, at Bream's Grove (South Oakwood Mine was situated there) and Noxon, to mention but a few. The Oakwood Levels were recorded in 1608 and in the early 19th century they were owned by David Mushet; the entrance to his Deep Level Mine, at the bottom of Mill Hill, can still be seen but with difficulty due to the undergrowth. In about 1826 he built the Oakwood Tramroad to service his mines. This branched off the Milkwall track after that had left Parkend and then, turning south some distance further on, passed in front of where the Parkend toll house was later built. The only glimpse of the tramroad is in a photograph of the toll house taken in 1888.

The tramroad travelled on up the valley towards Bream and some stone blocks can still be seen on the route as it heads towards the Flour Mill site. The remains of the Bromley Hill furnace, which dates from 1856 and belonged to the Ebbw Vale Steel & Iron Works Ltd, can be seen opposite Oakwood Mill; it was out of use by 1877. Further up the valley, known as China Bottom and leading towards the Noxon iron ore mines, were other pits – iron ore on the left and coal on the right. China Engine Mine also belonged to the Ebbw Vale Company and was probably worked for both iron and coal. The large shaft was capped but this had fallen in by 1993 and it was then open to the sky. More blocks can be found on the track behind the holding pool for the old Oakwood Mill, as the tramroad made its way to these latter mines.

Coal was first mined at Bream around 1750 but the deep mines came much later.

A group of miners at Flour Mill Colliery. Part of Princess Royal, these mines were a principal source of employment for Bream men for nearly 100 years. Flour Mill opened in 1869 and coal extraction finished in 1928 but it remained in use for ventilation purposes as it was connected underground to Princess Royal. This photograph was taken circa 1910; note several of the miners are wearing 'yorks', leather straps tied round their legs, just below the knee, to stop dust going up their trousers.

Bream shop adverts, 1935.

Flour Mill Colliery was sunk in 1872 and taken over by the Princess Royal Colliery in 1906, who then deepened it to allow working of the lower seams. It closed in 1931 and the buildings, together with those of the nearby Oakwood Chemical Works of 1844, were then used by the Ragosine Oil Company and now by Forest Lubricants Ltd. The fine engine house is now owned by Bill Parker. Flour Mill was connected to Princess Royal by a tram road, which ran under the Bream – Parkend Road by Navvies Arch. Princess Royal, on the Bream – Whitecroft road, was the dominating mine in the area, employing 1,138 men in 1922; it closed in 1962. The then modern building housing the pithead baths is now an outlet for H.J. Roberts, general dealers of Cinderford. The spoil heap below has been mostly levelled for hard core. As with other mines in the Forest, it was affected by the National Strike of 1921 and again in the General Strike of 1926.

As well as the deep mines, there were many small drift mines, worked by groups of miners, the spoil heaps of which were dotted round the village. Henry Robins, of Bream's Eaves, was granted a pit at that place in April 1844 *'about 50 yards in from the deep of a pit called Capel Quaz. Bounded on the deep by Knockley Tump Colliery.'* Earlier, in 1841, James Morse, Free Miner, of Bream Woodside, had the Uncertainty in Bream Grove, belonging to Pastor's Hill estate. Surface damage was caused to Pastor's Hill and Little Brockhollands estates in 1873, whilst as late as 1929 the owner of Pastor's Hill was awarded damages from the Little Brockhollands No. 2 Colliery, situated by the side of the lane leading from the Lydney road to the house. More pits and their spoil tips were dotted around some of the other fields but everything was cleared when the site was open-casted in the early 1980s.

Knockley quarries lay alongside the Bream – Parkend road. There was a tunnel beneath the road at the northern end, now blocked, which connected to the Oakwood branch tramway. Most of these quarries have been infilled since the last war. Also between Parkend Road and the Flour Mill were the Hang Hill quarries, closed a century ago. Despite protests from local residents, Gerald Morgan of Berry Hill was given permission in July 1998 to remove 1,200 tonnes of sandstone – without blasting or crushing – annually for ten years. The history of Dean's extractive industries still continues.

When studying the population of Bream over the centuries, it has to be remembered that the village was included with Newland, Clearwell, Le Bailey and Coleford, so that an exact figure cannot be given; Atkins records a total of 2,700 in 1712; Rudder, 2,997 in 1779; and Rudge, 2.543 in 1801. Sir Robert Atkins stated there were 60 families or 300 people in Bream in 1712 and he also mentioned there were a quota of miners and colliers in those places.

Bream Road, Forest of Dean

By 1831, the Newland, Clearwell and Bream tithings recorded 1,745 inhabitants, this having risen to 2,316 in 1861, most of the increase being in Bream and due to mining. Later census numbers for Bream alone give 907 in 1871, 2,013 for 1885, 2,429 in 1901, 2,524 in 1911 and 2,649 in 1931, with about 3,200 in the latest survey in 1989.

The Maypole in 1911. It stood about 40 feet high, had a weather vane at its peak and was the only one in the Forest but was removed circa 1925 being deemed a traffic hazard. Rumour has it the local doctor ran into on one occasion, having enjoyed too much home-made wine given to him by grateful patients. The shops on the left were Mr and Mrs Cannock's general store, with Richard Heighways grocery beyond, which had also once been the post office; it later became the police station. All the buildings on the left, up as far as the New Inn, were demolished in the 1960s for road widening. The house behind the Maypole, Elsmore's Farm, was once the Live and Let Live Inn.

The High Street, looking towards the site of the Maypole, in the late 1930s. Dunham's bakery and Chilton's, tobacconists and confectioners, can be seen on the left, whilst the building jutting out just past the telegraph pole was Bream's first police station; the New Inn is behind and the Cross Keys is opposite. Cross Keys farm, demolished a few years after this to make way for Cross Keys garage, is behind the wall on the right. A solitary motor car can just be made out down by the junction but it was still safe at this period for an old 'un to stroll in the road.

Bream Village

The years roll by at the Maypole end of the High Street. The first view, above, is looking across the Lydney to Coleford road and dates from around 1908. Heighway's grocers is on the right, whilst the boy leaning aginst the Maypole is Norman Schlosberg, whose father Charlie ran a drapers shop further up the High Street. The photograph below, taken by the Coleford photographer F.N. Jones, dates from 1906. On the Maypole is a tattered poster advertising Bream Fruit & Vegetable Show, which took place on 11 August of that year. The entrance to the Cross Keys Inn can be seen on the left; note the sign promoting the delights of the Stroud Brewery Company's ales, which they sold. The New Inn on the right was run at the time of this picture by A. Hewlett and he was followed as licensee by E.H. Birt. The single storey shop in front of it was Camm's butchers in the mid 1920s.

HIGH STREET BREAM

The 1930s scene above shows a few subtle changes had taken place; telegraph poles had arrived, the road had been made up, acquiring pavements and a white line, and Cannock's tobacconists and newsagents on the right had been given a facelift – Mr Cannock can be seen outside. The little boy in the middle of the road on his bike would still have been quite safe though. By the 1950s, below, he would have had to be more careful; a couple of cars can be seen and the Cross Keys garage has appeared, complete with rustic shelter for the pumps, on the site of the farmyard. The garage sold Fina petrol, another name now consigned to history. Camm's has become an antiques and second-hand furniture shop – note the armchair outside, no doubt positioned so the proprietor could enjoy a little of the late afternoon sun – and Cannock's, just out of view right, was now the police station.

Looking up the High Street from the New Inn in the early 1930s. Note the Cross Keys also offered afternoon teas. Beyond is the farmyard and buildings which were cleared to make way for the Cross Keys garage. Downham's bakery is on the right, with their two Morris delivery vans parked outside. This postcard is one of an extensive and interesting series of the Forest by R.G. Gibbs of Cinderford.

The top of the High Street in the 1930s – note the ladies' fashions in particular. Lloyds Bank is on the left, housed in a little office at one end of the Williams & Cottons store beyond. In the 1960s it moved into purpose built premises nearby which it still occupies although opening hours are restricted. The Two Swans Inn, referred to irreverently by locals as 'The Double Ducks', is opposite, the licensee at the time of the photograph being Jimmy Price. Beyond the pub can be seen Taylor's shop, Meek's outfitters with the drawn blinds, Mountjoy's general store, which had been established at these premises since at least 1889, and, lastly, Charlie Schlosberg's drapery. The man in the street is 'Popeye' Davis, one of the local teachers and amongst the four ladies is Mrs Kate Rudge.

Bream Miners' Welfare Cinema in 1952. The first cinema in the village was a long wooden hut next to the Pike House, in which silent movies were shown before the First World War. It was requistioned by the army and taken away around 1916. The Miners' Welfare Hall was built in 1927, and used for social functions and dances before becoming a cinema in 1939. It was altered towards the end of the war, the seating being reversed so that the best seats became those up on the stage, where the screen had previously been sited. It always seemed to be bitterly cold inside so filmgoers had to wrap up warmly to watch their favourite stars. It was almost entirely destroyed by fire in June 1946 but was rebuilt, reopening in August 1947. Films ceased to be shown around the mid 1950s and the hall was taken over by Bream Rugby Club in 1960; the building's front has since been heavily extended. Lest anyone think the cinema merely showed 'shorts' and 'B' movies, the programme for January 1952 is on the left. Disney's *Cinderella, King Solomon's Mines* and big John Wayne in *Operation Pacific* – these were top class movies and even today's generation will have heard of some of them! Mr. A. Brookes, Secretary of the Miners Welfare Committee which ran the cinema, was justifiably proud of the films he had to offer – '*We challenge any Cinema in the Country to produce a better line up of pictures in one month*' he wrote on the reverse of the programme.

PROGRAMME FOR JANUARY, 1952

Thursday, January 3rd   Three Days

VICTOR MATURE AND HEDY LAMARR
in
SAMSON AND DELILAH
Biblical Story.   In Technicolor

Monday, January 7th   Three Days

RANDOLPH SCOTT AND VICTOR JORY
in
FIGHTING MAN OF THE PLAINS
Western Thriller.   In Technicolor.

Thursday, January 10th   Three Days

DEBORAH KERR AND STEWART GRANGER
in
KING SOLOMON'S MINES
Rider Haggard's Classic.   In Technicolor.

Monday, January 14th   Three Days

"LASSIE" AND PAUL KELLY
in
THE PAINTED HILLS
In Technicolor.
also YOU BELONG TO MY HEART
In Technicolor.

Thursday, January 17th   Three Days

DAVID NIVEN AND VERA ELLEN
in
HAPPY GO LOVELY
Great Musical Romance.   In Technicolor.

Monday, January 21st   Three Days

JOHN WAYNE AND PATRICIA NEAL
in
OPERATION PACIFIC
Thrilling Submarine Drama.

Thursday, January 24th   Three Days

HOWARD KEEL AND BETTY HUTTON
in
ANNIE GET YOUR GUN
Western Musical Romance.   In Technicolor.

Monday, January 28th   Three Days

Walt Disney's Masterpiece

CINDERELLA
For Children of all Ages.   In Technicolor.

The Rising Sun Inn, today the only one of Bream's public houses still open in its original premises, albeit now renamed The Village Inn. The year 1729 appears over the small window right above the entrance door; this may just be a building date rather than indicating when it opened but it was certainly an inn by 1787. Many events were held in the long room on the right, including political meetings and, in the 1930s when it was all the rage, roller skating. The inn also had its own Friendly Society. This photograph dates from about 1907 and publican Charles Morse is stood in the entrance with his wife, a serving maid and a few regulars.

Arnold Perret's brewery dray is seen here making a delivery to the Rising Sun from their store next to Lydney Town station, around 1912. From 1910, Arnold Morse became the third member of the family to run the pub – an earlier relative, Thomas, had been landlord in the 1870s and 80s – and he was still landlord in 1919. Note the Pike House down the hill just beyond the horse and cart; when erected in the 19th century it would have been on the outskirts of the then village.

The same view 25 years later; a Red & White bus passes through on a service from Coleford to Lydney, via Bream and Whitecroft, with a solitary horse and cart coming the other way. The Rising Sun had been under the stewardship of Joseph Dufty since the early 1920s and his wife Anne, 'Aunty Annie' to regulars, was a popular landlady, although renowned as a stern, no nonsense type with rowdy drinkers. The loss of the trees on the left has radically altered this view today.

Looking back up the High Street, circa 1910, with the Pike House prominent on the left. Bream Institute is opposite but out of sight, as is the wooden shed just past the Pike House, which acted as the village's first cinema. Lewis's shop and the rising Sun Inn can be seen up the road on the left and William's & Cottons grocery store is facing down the hill; later it became a Miles's general hardware store and latterly it was Robin's Nest, specialising in baby clothes and accessories; at the time of writing the shop is empty. The Pike House may have been built in 1828 along with the road to Parkend or in 1859, at the same time as the road from Bream to Yorkley was constructed. It ceased to function as a toll collection point from 31 October 1888, as did all the other local pike houses, when the Dean Forest Turnpike Trust was abolished. It was then run as a sweet shop for many years by a lady called Barbara Hunt. Unfortunately, it was demolished some decades ago.

High Street circa 1905, before the Co-op was built at the top of Whitecroft Road. Bristol House is on the right; in the 1930s it was Ben Bath's bakery and is now a private house. Ben Bath had the tragic distinction of becoming the first man from Bream to be killed in World War Two, in Norway. Oakleigh, a private residence, and Britannia House, home to Williams & Cottons drapery, are further down on the right; Oakleigh is now Bream Pharmacy, whilst Britannia House was a pottery in the 1950s and 60s, and is now Farmer & Clark insurance brokers. Note the muddy unmade road.

Four ladies in their Edwardian finery stroll arm in arm down High Street in about 1910 – the dirt road must have played havoc with the bottoms of their dresses! Manchester House is on the right, on the corner of the road leading to Brockhollands, and in front of it is the Hard-up Tree, so called because the miners used to gather round it during times of short working or strikes. Note the lack of pavements and the number of trees on the green by the old Jubilee Well, long gone as is the Hard-up Tree, which was cut down, supposedly accidentally, in the 1950s.

Bream schools around 1910, with a group of men, probably miners in their Sunday best, gathered around the crossroads, near the Hard-up Tree. On the right is the Church of England School, with the recently built Infants School through the trees on the left.

The Infants School pictured around 1912, looking quite new. Built of Forest stone, it opened in 1907 and was provided because the C of E School opposite had become overcrowded. By the time of this view it had already been renamed Bream Council School and the attendance was over 300. Pupils of the 1930s will recall Miss Young was the headmistress. The building, much enlarged over the years, has been through many changes during the 20th century but, as Bream C of E (Voluntary Controlled) Primary School, it is still in operation for teaching the younger local children.

Class 4 Infants, circa 1910. They would be about 8 years old so the lad in the back row must have been very tall for his age! The girls look pretty in white smocks, and the boys very smart in jackets and wing collars. Teachers Mr J. Mullen and Miss Polly Williams look suitably proud of their charges.

Bream schoolgirls in the High Street in 1908 – the boys appear to have been kept in the background. Although the postcard is captioned 'Play-time', it is unlikely they were normally allowed out to play in the street; most likely this gathering was for photographic purposes. The card was published by Mr A. Batten who at that time ran the Post Office in Bream. Note the picture was taken prior to the construction of Manchester House and the Hard-up Tree thus stands in splendid isolation in the centre background, with the C of E School behind it also more clearly visible.

Bream boys in the 1930s. Amongst the boys are Bobby Worgan, Geoff Wilden, Michael and Alan Hirst, Cyril Gifford and Dave Rogers, whilst the teachers are Mr. Watson and Doris Worgan.

High St. Bream

BEMI

A few minor changes had taken place by the time of this mid 1950s view. The road was metalled, pavements had been provided and the Hard-up Tree had gone. The trees still flourished on the green and a swing had been placed in their shade for the children to play on. The sylvan charm these trees afforded the centre of the village has today been lost as, most unfortunately, the majority of them have been cut down. The shop on the corner, Manchester House, was now occupied by James & Son, ladies fashions; next door to it was a confectioners. Note Camm's van on the extreme right.

A view from 1909 showing the trees in process of being cut down so construction of the Co-op could begin on the corner of Whitecroft Road and Parkend Road. The Methodist chapel of 1851 was extended on the right in 1859 and, just below it down the hill, is Hirst's shop.

Hirst Bros, grocers, drapers and general store, in about 1908, with J.E. Hirst, the author's grandfather, stood in the doorway. Reputed to be one of the oldest established businesses in the village, in the early 1930s grocery deliveries were made around the locality by horse and cart – Fred Robins being the driver, with 'Tom', a bay, hauling the cart. Note the drape to protect the fabrics inside the shop from the sun, the shutters on the right, ready to place over the windows at closing time, the good supply of galvanised buckets and the display of 'Daffodil' soap in the window. The grocery was latterly run by D.K. Dell. The premises are no longer a shop but home to MJP Publications.

Parkend Road in the early 1900s. On the right is Will Smith's butchers shop. It was later taken over by Roy Hutchence, who ran a motor cycle repair business from the premises before coverting it into a private residence, which it still is today.

Above is a 1935 advert for 'Vera', ladies hairstylist and beautician, who operated from Lydney and Parkend Road. Maurice Wright's greengrocery in Parkend Road closed in the late 1980s, at the time of the photograph, left. Below is an advert for his shop, also from 1935.

The village expanded in the 1920s and 30s with the construction of council houses down Parkend Road, as this late 1930s view shows; many of them are now privately owned. Knockley Woods is in the middle distance and the New Fancy Colliery dirt tips appear on the skyline.

Bream post office was in the High Street, opposite Highfield Avenue. Originally it had been in Heighway's shop at the Maypole but moved here in the late 1890s into Alfred Batten's grocery. Later it was run by the Gatfields and then the Selbys but it closed in the late 1980s and is now Bream Auto Store. A new post office has since opened at Family Affair in Brockhollands Road but mail now receives an anonymous 'Gloucestershire' postmark, the Bream mark having gone. On the left are examples of Bream letter and parcel post postmarks from the 1930s.

The post office in Parkend Road closed in 1994, despite a campaign by villagers to keep it open, following the death of Post Mistress Millicent Adams who had operated it for over 40 years; one of her staff, Tessa Elliott, also put in 45 years service there.

No date is known for the original erection of St. James's church, the earliest recorded mention being when it was reseated by the Donning family in 1618. Between 1822 and 1826 it was rebuilt by the Rev. Henry Poole and has been altered and enlarged several times since. The picture above dates from about 1912, whilst the interior view, left, is a few years earlier and shows the church decorated with flowers – possibly at Easter judging by the crosses. Following the 1981 fire which severely damaged the interior, photographs such as this are quite important now. The final picture below, is an unusual aspect of the church, looking along the Lydney to Coleford road in the early 1930s.

James Church, Bream.

Some of the properties along the Coleford Road; Ferndale Cottage, above, pictured in the 1920s, is opposite the church and is now called just Dale Cottage. It was the home of J.H. Fewings, the author's maternal grandfather. Left, and also a 1920s view, is The Breezes, the author's family home, owned by her father Dyson Hirst. Below is another of Bream's disappearing pubs The Olde Winding Wheel, previously the Miners' Arms. It was first recorded in the late 1870s and closed in the early 1990s. The building has since been turned into flats. Meanwhile, this busy, narrow and dangerous stretch of road awaits widening improvements, which are currently on hold due to old mine workings beneath. Legend has it that 100 years ago it was possible to walk underground from Mill Hill, beneath the church, to The Shravers, about 1,000 yards south of Maypole garage. Indeed, old shafts are indicated in this area on the map on the inside front cover.

The view, top left, is Brockhollands Road in the early 1950s. Just peeking into the left of the picture is the end of Raglan Villa, which has since been converted into a rest home for the elderly called The High Anchorage. Whilst no further building has taken place along this stretch of lane, the height of the hedgerows would prevent a similar view being taken today. The house shown top right, is The Laurels, at Bream Woodside. This and the following two photographs were in a collection with the Rechabite pictures on page 30, so they would all date from around 1911 and the houses featured are likely to be the homes of local abstainers. Centre right is Nos. 1 and 2 Claremont Villas; note the pristine appearance of the stonework, indicating they were constructed probably about ten years before the picture was taken. The bottom view shows Vine Tree Cottage. It still stands today – it is currently the home of Mrs Alice Cook – whilst the lane on which it sits is now called Hang Hill Road; the whole area was once just known as Mill Hill but road names have since been added, no doubt to make life easier for the post office and emergency services.

The Hodges family are quite well known in Bream and Dave Hodges bungalow is built on the site of the first cinema. This lady is his grandmother, Mrs. 'Bib' Lewis, who ran a general store in the High Street and which is now the Central Stores. Her husband later had a fish shop in the adjoining building, as the advertisement above, from 1935, indicates.

Mr. and Mrs. W. J. Holder are seen right in their motor cycle and sidecar combination, outside his blacksmith's shop in the High Street. It was situated opposite Downham's Bakery amnd was later used by T. J. Watkins as his builders' yard. Demolished in the mid 1980s, the site is now occupied by a bungalow.

The picture on the left shows Frank Downham and Mr. Lodge in the doorway to the bakery in the 1920s. The sign above the window reads 'The Forest Bakers', a statement reflected in their advertising as illustrated above. Note the hoist for lifting the sacks of flour straight up into the storage loft. This loft entrance was bricked up in later years, although the beam supporting the hoist remained jutting out of the wall till the end. Downham's Forest Bakery finally closed in 1988 and the bake house depicted here has been demolished. A list of their customers from before the First World War, which the author has a copy of, reads like a 'Who's Who' of Bream! There was also a grocer's shop attached to the bakery, on the right, which today is occupied by a restaurant, Chef's Forest Fodder.

~ 29 ~

"Progress" Tent, I.O.R. Bream. July 1911.

Rechabites with a future. Bream. '11.

The Rechabites are a Temperance society, one of many which flourished in the country in the Victorian and Edwardian eras. Formed initially to try and modify the effect that alcohol played in peoples lives, many of these organisations soon became friendly societies as well. The size of their memberships and the funds that were generated could thus be used to control the lives of those who joined, thereby keeping them away from the 'demon drink' and to generally lead upstanding lives. It should be remembered that this was pre television and radio, an era when pubs were meeting places where folk spent much of their time outside work (hence the great number of such establishments in comparison to today), and alcohol was drunk routinely by farm labourers in the field and imbibed in quantity by miners anxious to wash away the mouthfuls of coal dust they took in every day. As such, drunkeness in some areas was almost routine. The Rechabites are still in existence today but these views show a Gloucester District meeting at Bream in July 1911. The family on the left are the Fewings, father J.H. with son Norman and daughter Marjorie. Below are some of the banners. Note the caption to the picture of the babies – 'Rechabites with a future.'

Gloucester District, No 12.

~ 30 ~

A group of WW1 reservists photographed at Ferndale, Bream, home of J.H. Fewings – abstainer, J.P. and the sergeant sitting in the centre of the front row. Fifth from left, back row, is Dyson Hirst (3rd Devon Regt), whilst further along, one from the right, is Norman Fewings, seen previously when a little younger at the Rechabites gathering but here a member of the Inns of Court Officer Training Corps. Front third from left is thought to be Mr Cannock, who owned the newsagents at the Maypole.

BREAM WAR MEMORIAL
1914-18

A. Brookes	J. Kent	W.H. Pearce
A Dodgshon	E. Kilby	A.E. Thomas
E. Evans	L. Lodge	H. Waslay
P. Frowen	E. Lucas	A. Watkins
H.L. Howells	J. Matty	O. Wolks
T. Jones	L. Mayne	E. Worgan
W.T. Kear	G. Nelmes	G. Wynn

1939-45

N. Baker	W. Drew	C. Morgan
M. Bath	E. Grindle	J. Neilson
R. Carpenter	D. Hancocks	J. Overington
T. Challenger	V. James	T. Turley
L. Court	D. Jenkins	W. Wildin
W. Crote	C. Marshall	S. Wilks
D. Davies	P. Meek	D. Wintle
S. Drew	R. Moore	
Doreen Brookes		Dorothy Hancocks

The War Memorial erected on the Sun Tump in 1921-2 in memory of those who gave their lives in the First World War. The memorial was modelled on the cenotaph in Whitehall and said to be the only such one. Note the names of the fallen have not as yet been added in this early 1920s view. After the Second World War, those who died during that conflict were added to the memorial; as the list shows, it included two women from the village. In 1995 a plaque was dedicated to the Burma Star Association.

The funeral procession of Norman Watkins, who died aged 26 in 1936, some months after being injured whilst playing rugby, seen trooping past the Rising Sun. Note women rarely attended funerals in pre-war days.

LYDNEY, _____ June 17 191 2

We beg to advise you that the following Wagons have to-day been consigned to your order :—

NO.	WEIGHT		QUALITY	DESTINATION
8	8 16	}	Steam	J. Acton
12	8 0			
4	8 16		"	Warmley
2	8 10		"	Bitton

PRINCESS ROYAL COLLIERY CO., Ltd.

Although first galed in 1843, it was not until the Princess Royal Colliery Co took over in 1891 that major development took place at Flour Mill Colliery, above. It was connected to their other pit, the nearby Park Gutter, by a tramway, coal being hauled down it in horse drawn wagons for loading into railway trucks at the screens there. After they were connected underground for drainage and ventilation purposes, coal finally ceased to be wound at Flour Mill in 1928 and the surviving buildings are now home to an oil supply business and Bill Parker's engineering works where steam locomotives are repaired and refurbished. Left, is a Princess Royal Co coal consignment advice postcard of 1912. Park Gutter Colliery, below, survived until 1962 and. after the closure of Flour Mill, was always known as Princess Royal. This classic view down the hill would be as most locals remember it, with the workmen's bus in the car park and the railway bridge, carrying the branch from Tuft's Junction into the mine, at the bottom.

At one time, two thirds of the men of Bream worked for the Princess Royal Company, at Flour Mill or Park Gutter – nearly 1,200 were employed there in the mid 1920s. As such any fluctuations in work, due to economic or political considerations, affected the village deeply. Coal mining was a hard and dirty profession, whilst collieries were privately owned businesses run for profit, so it was inevitable there would be clashes from time to time. The National Strike of 1921 brought Forest miners out but the subsequent lockout and the lack of support from other workers led to many men soon going back to work. The top picture shows strike breakers under police escort at Flour Mill Colliery in 1921. The unsatisfactory outcome of this strike led on to the General Strike of 1926 and the subsequent lockout of striking miners, which brought whole communities into conflict with the mine owners and the Government.

The lockout lasted seven months, before the miners eventually were defeated, and many families existed on starvation rations supplemented by whatever they could grow, scrounge, steal or were given. The middle view shows food parcels being handed out at Bream in 1926. The only creatures to gain any respite at these times were the pit ponies, who were brought to the surface. They also came up during the miners' holiday period and the bottom view shows ponies from Princess Royal enjoying their summer break on Saunders Green, in the early 1950s.

Princess Royal Colliery and General View. Bream.

Despite its industrial background, the Forest of Dean has always been blessed with beautiful vistas, as this view across the Whitecroft valley from Bream shows. The scattered communities of Pillowell and Yorkley sprawl across the slopes in the far distance, whilst a plume of steam marks the position of Princess Royal Colliery at the bottom. This early 1930s postcard view is once again the work of R.G. Gibbs of Cinderford.

Mill. Bream.

The top view shows Mill Hill in the early 1930s, looking from The Tufts. The photographer (Mr Gibb again!) was standing in front of the hut where the band practices and the cenotaph is just off to the right. The field in the centre is now the football pitch. The next photograph, right centre upper, is looking from the Breezes around the same time. Elsmore's farm is at the front, on the left, with the New Inn and the Cross Keys just beyond, and New Road in the background. The picture below is a similar view but taken from a little farther back, showing the fields which are now covered by the Maypole Green estate. The field on the right was used for fairs and circuses, the entrance being either from High Street (below Downhams) or just past the row of houses above Well Meadow, in Lydney Lane, where the Giffords and the Wicks lived. The pole in the centre is a radio mast. Finally, the bottom picture was taken in the winter of 1951 when Forest Road was being made up; note the workmens' hut above the old quarry. The house below is Bay Tree Cottage where Dr. Grew lived; he was owner and first editor of *Working Sheepdog News*.

Bream Football Club circa 1910. Identified are Albert Jones and F.B. Hirst, who are respectively fifth and seventh from the left in the front row. Boots with steel toecaps and baggy shorts for the players, and a ball that weighed a ton to start with and then got even heavier on a soggy pitch – not the same game as today but there was no arguing with the ref either! Matches were played on a field loaned by Sam Wildin, which lay just behind the church.

Bream Thursday Cricket Club, season 1910. The photographer, once again F.N. Jones of Coleford, also recorded the names of those pictured. Back row, from left to right: R. Shingles, L. Jenkins, A. Jenkins, F.S. Watkins, D. Hirst and the Rev. G.W.L. Cass. Front row: F. Mullan, F. Blower, H. Yarworth, F.B. Hirst, Capt. A. Robins, P. Baldwin and W. Wathen. Because these men worked on Saturdays, they played on their half day off from work – Thursday afternoons, early closing, hence the name of the club!

The cricket team in the early 1950s. Back row, from left to right: Denby Adams, Grantley Parfitt, Cyril Gifford, Don Sims, Eric Cooper and Gwyn Johnston. Front: Alan Hirst, Norman Cooper, Cliff Cooper, John James and Jack Wildin. Alan Hirst was the son of F.B. Hirst, seen above; he took over the running of the family shop in the 1950s. John James, who only passed away recently, owned a well known furnishings business in the High Street, which is now run by his widow.

Bream
Rugby Football
1878-1978

BREAM R.F.C

Centenary Fixture
Programme 1978-79

The Forest has always been predominently a rugby area and Bream has long been one of its centres, as the centenary fixture list front cover, reproduced above, indicates. At one time there were five teams in the area but, over the years, they amalgamated to form Bream Rugby Club. In 1960 the old Miners Welfare Cinema was bought for £1,800 and, after refurbishment, was opened two years later as the new rugby club headquarters. The club fields four teams, as well as Junior and Mini rugby sides. The 1905/6 team is pictured, top, along with a trophy captured in that season. Below, on the right, is the team of season 1957/8, with the Forest Combination Cup won that year.

Fun and games! Bream Rugby Club held a Married Men's Match on 3 April 1909, the players taking part in fancy dress. The result is not known but no doubt it was a high scoring game, played out with much hilarity.

The rugby club dinner is a highlight on the village's social calendar. This photograph was taken at one such event in the 1950s, with, in front from left to right, Sam Stone, Tom Birt, Harold Watkins, Jimmy Edmunds and John Gunter, whilst opposite them are Rupert Daw, Charlie Brice and Tom Davey. Behind them is Frank Green.

Sam Wildin, who let the football team play on one his fields, lived with his family at Court Farm. A 17th century farmhouse, the plaster and whitewash shown here has since been removed to reveal the original stonework, and it still belongs to the Wildin family. Mrs Sam Wildin and daughter are seen in this 1920s photograph.

The Hirsts having long been a part of the village and the author raided the family album for some of these pictures; this is her grandfather J.E. Hirst, photographed harrowing Top Meadow, Pastor's Hill, in the 1920s. The cottages in the background have been demolished and in their place today are two bungalows, 'Mayfair' and 'Alameida'. The area on the left is Colliers Beech.

An idyllic farming scene at The Blistors in 1938. R.V. Jones, who also owned a butchers shop in the village, is preparing to go haymaking with 'Lassie' – the horse, a thoroughbred Hackney mare, was actually officially named 'Dagmar's Daughter Grace'. She was 29 years old when this picture was taken and had been in France during the First World War. The mower was 30 years old too.

Dipping day for the sheep, in August 1958, with Mr F. Preece of Dark Hole Farm bringing his flock down through the village, near the institute. Harold Watkins is in the car. Note the tin building in the background, part of which was Riley Lewis's shoe shop, whilst the rest was a greengrocers. The Rising Sun is beyond.

RILEY LEWIS, HIGH ST., BREAM

If your "Soles" are worn, come and be "Heeled."
"Operations" carried out daily.

High-Class Boot and Shoe Repair Service.

Three photographs taken during the incidence of a fire at Treherne's Farm in 1958. The top view is looking along what is now Beech Way, with the entrance to the farm on the left marked by the fire appliances. The bottom views show firemen damping down the straw in the barn which caught fire; the cow ignores the commotion, seeming far more interested in having her picture taken!

A rare glimpse of the Oakwood Inn in the mid 1950s. It was situated at the bottom of Mill Hill on the road to Clements End and was recorded as a corn mill from 1520, later becoming an inn until sometime in the mid 1960s, when it closed. It is now a private house. The tramway to China Bottom ran up the valley behind it and across the road towards the Flour Mill are the remains of Bromley Hill Furnace.

A modern photograph of Pastor's Hill House, built in the 17th century but with later 20th century additions. One of the most historic houses in the village, it was once the home of James and Mary Gough, the benefactors of Bream church and also related to the Goughs who owned the New Inn at the same period.

Bibliography and sources

Bream Through the Ages, Vols. 1 & 2.	W.A. Camm
Old Industrial Sites of Wyedean.	A.G.R. Cross
The Commoner of Dean Forest.	C. Hart
Regard of the Forest of Dean in 1282.	C. Hart
Victoria County History of the County of Gloucester Vol. V. The Forest of Dean.	Ed. by N. Herbert
Forest of Dean.	Revd. H.G. Nicholls
Personalities of the Forest of Dean.	Revd. H.G. Nicholls
The Severn & Wye Railway Vol I.	I. Pope, P. Karau & R. How
Bream Church magazines 1901-2.	Revd. E.F. Eales

Parkend Road Methodist Church Jubilee Brochure 1906-1966; Wesleyan Church, Woodside, 1860-1959; G.J. Harris Directories; Kellys Directories; The Forester; The Dean Forest & Wye Valley Review; The New Regard (Local History Society Journal – various dates); Dean Archaeological Group Journal (various dates).